Other books by Lee J. Ames

DRAW 50 FAMOUS STARS

Lee J. Ames

DRAW
50
FAMOUS
STARS

*as selected by Rona Barrett's **Hollywood** magazine*

Doubleday & Company, Inc.
Garden City, New York

Library of Congress Catalog Card Number 81-43238
ISBN: 0-385-15688-X Trade
ISBN: 0-385-15689-8 Prebound
Copyright © 1982 by Lee J. Ames and Murray D. Zak
All Rights Reserved
Printed in the United States of America
First Edition

To Jocelyn, superstar

Many thanks to Holly Moylan for all her help

TO THE READER

This book will show you a way to draw faces. You need not start with the first illustration. Choose whichever you wish. When you have decided, follow the step-by-step method shown. *Very lightly* and *carefully,* sketch out the first step. However, this step, which seems the easiest, should be done *most carefully.* Step number two is added to step number one, also lightly and also very carefully. Step number three is sketched right on top of numbers one and two. Continue this way to the last step.

It may seem strange to ask you to be extra careful when you are drawing what seem to be the easiest first steps, but this is most important, for a careless mistake at the beginning may spoil the whole picture at the end. As you sketch out each step, watch the spaces between the lines, and see that they are the same. After each step, you may want to lighten your work by pressing it with a kneaded eraser (available at art supply stores).

When you have finished, you may want to reinforce the final step in India ink with a fine brush or pen. When the ink is dry, use the kneaded eraser to clean off the pencil lines. The eraser will not affect the India ink.

Here are some suggestions: In the first few steps, even when all seems quite correct, you might do well to hold your work up to a mirror. Sometimes the mirror shows that you've twisted the drawing off to one side without being aware of it. At first you may find it difficult to draw the egg shapes, or ball shapes, or sausage shapes, or just to make the pencil go where you wish. Don't be discouraged. The more you practice, the more control you will develop.

In drawing these portraits I made extensive use of photographs. Most professional illustrators do use photographic help. Some artists may "remember" sufficient details of an occasional face to enable them to create a reasonable resemblance. But this happens rarely and is never as successful as when a model or photograph is used.

The only equipment you'll need will be a medium or soft pencil, paper, the kneaded eraser, and, if you wish, a compass, pen or brush.

The first steps in this book are shown darker than necessary so they can be clearly seen. (Keep your work very light.)

Remember there are many other ways and methods to make drawings. This book shows just one method. Why don't you seek out other ways from teachers, from libraries and, most important . . . from inside yourself?

Lee J. Ames

TO THE PARENT OR TEACHER

"David can draw a face better than anybody else!" Such peer acclaim and encouragement generate incentive. Contemporary methods of art instruction (freedom of expression, experimentation, self-evaluation of competence and growth) provide a vigorous, fresh-air approach for which we must all be grateful.

New ideas need not, however, totally exclude the old. One such is the "follow me, step-by-step" approach. In my young learning days this method was so common, and frequently so exclusive, that the student became nothing more than a pantographic extension of the teacher. In those days it was excessively overworked.

This does not mean that the young hand is never to be guided. Rather, specific guiding is fundamental. Step-by-step guiding that produces satisfactory results is valuable even when the means of accomplishment are not fully understood by the student.

The novice with a musical instrument is frequently taught to play simple melodies as quickly as possible, well before he learns the most elemental scratchings at the surface of music theory. The resultant self-satisfaction, pride in accomplishment, can be a significant means of providing motivation. And all from mimicking an instructor's "Do-as-I-do. . . ."

Mimicry is prerequisite for developing creativity.

We learn the use of tools by mimicry. Then we can use those tools for creativity. To this end I would offer the budding artist the opportunity to memorize or mimic the making of "pictures." "Pictures" he has been eager to be able to draw.

The use of this book should be available to anyone who *wants* to try another way of flapping his wings. Perhaps he will then get off the ground when his friend says, "David can draw a face better than anybody else!

Lee J. Ames

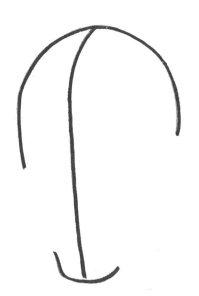
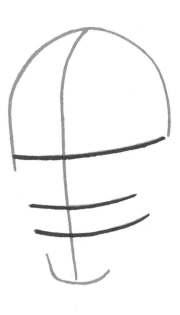

Telly Savalas

Jane Fonda

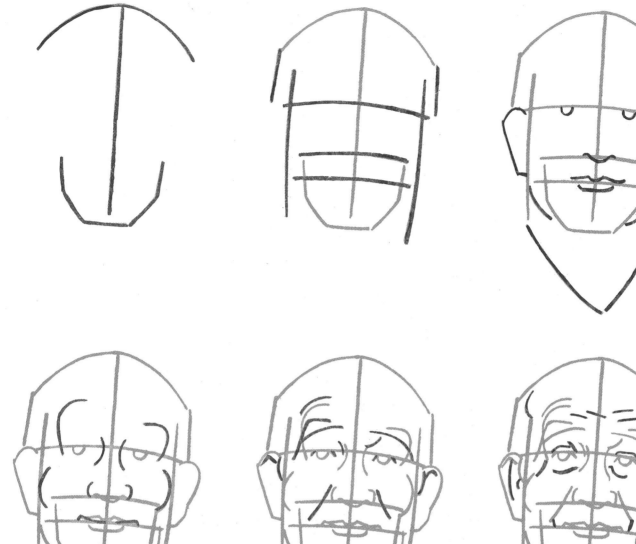

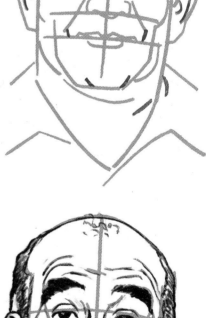

Edward Asner

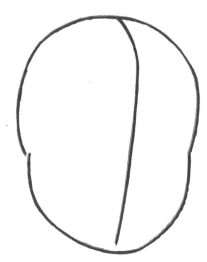
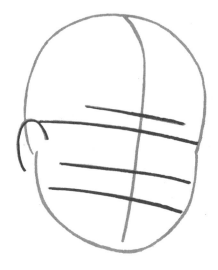
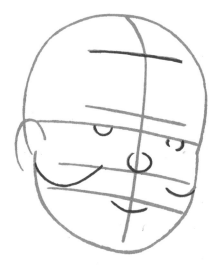
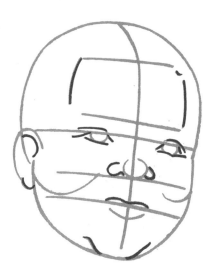
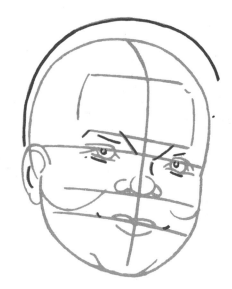

Gary Coleman

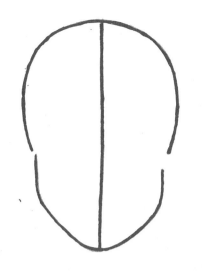
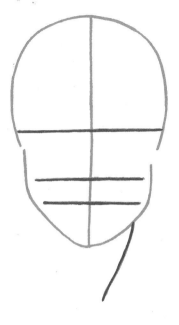
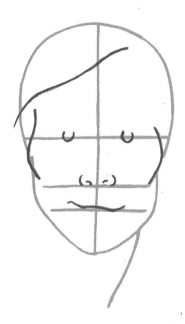
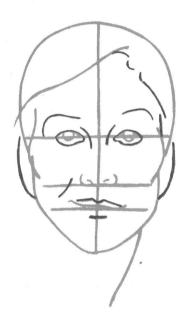
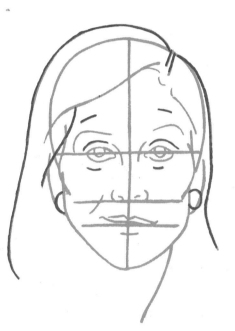

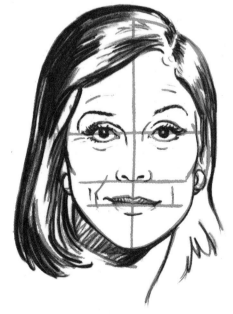

Mary Tyler Moore

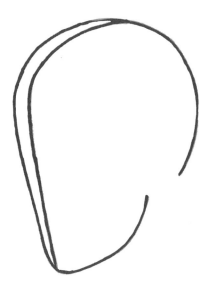
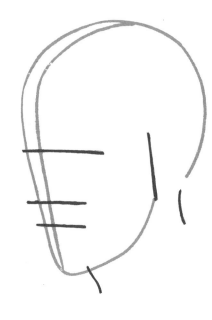
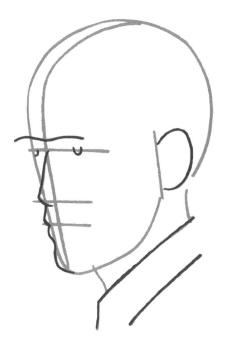

Sammy Davis, Jr.

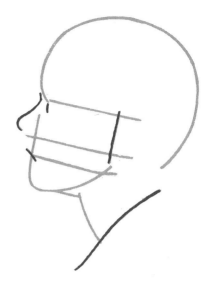
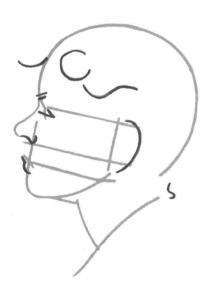

Ingrid Bergman

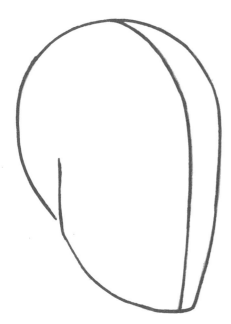
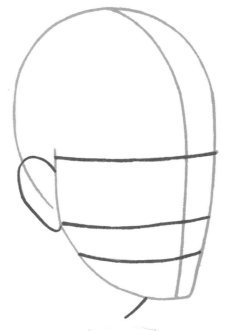
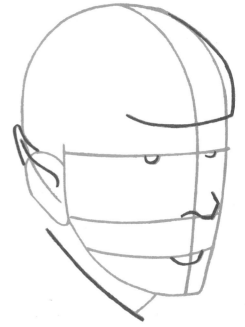
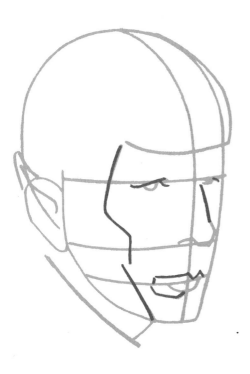

Leonard Nimoy

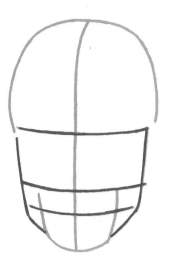
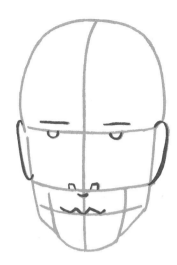
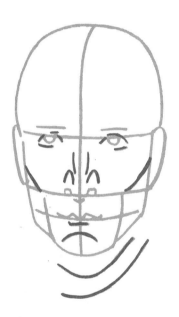
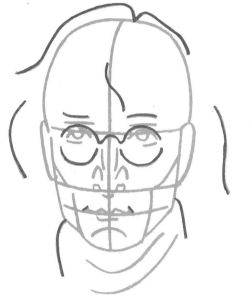

John Lennon

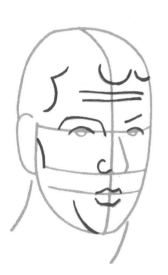

Billy Joel

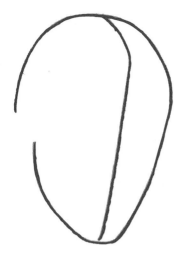

Olivia Newton-John

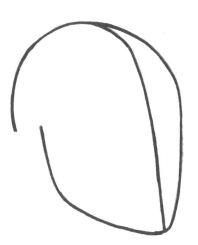
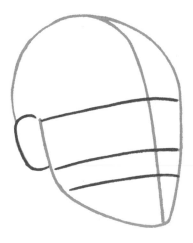
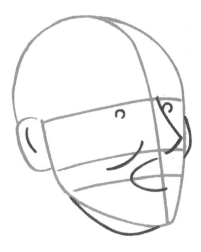
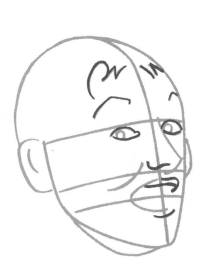

Phyllis Diller

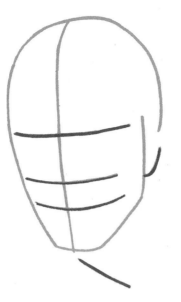
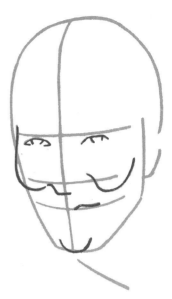
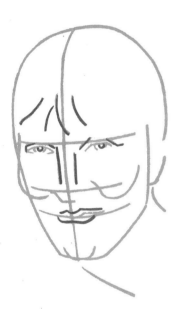

Rod Stewart

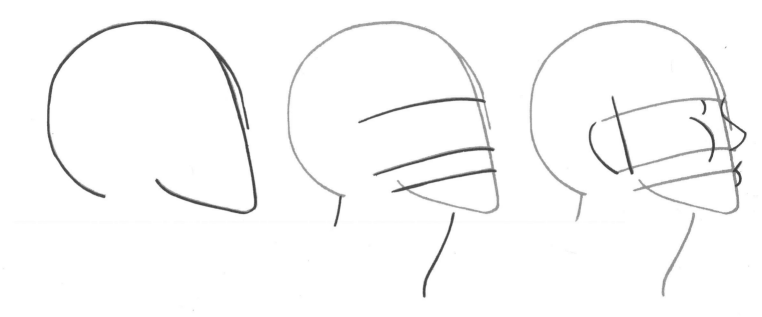

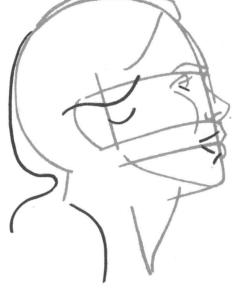

Liv Ullman

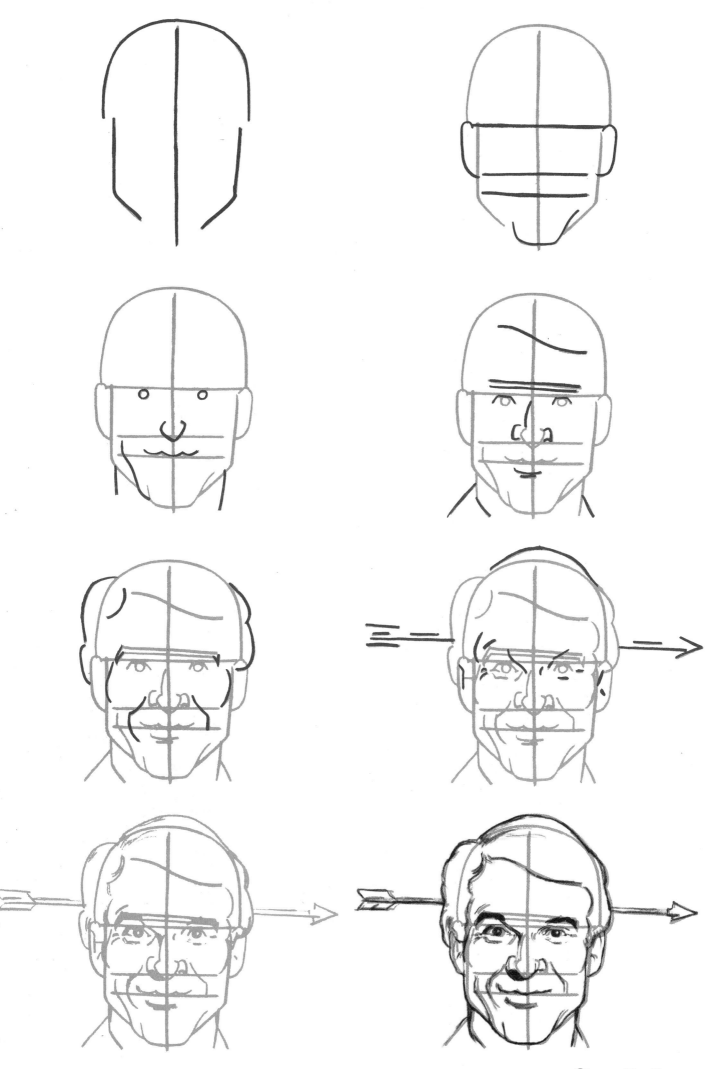

Steve Martin

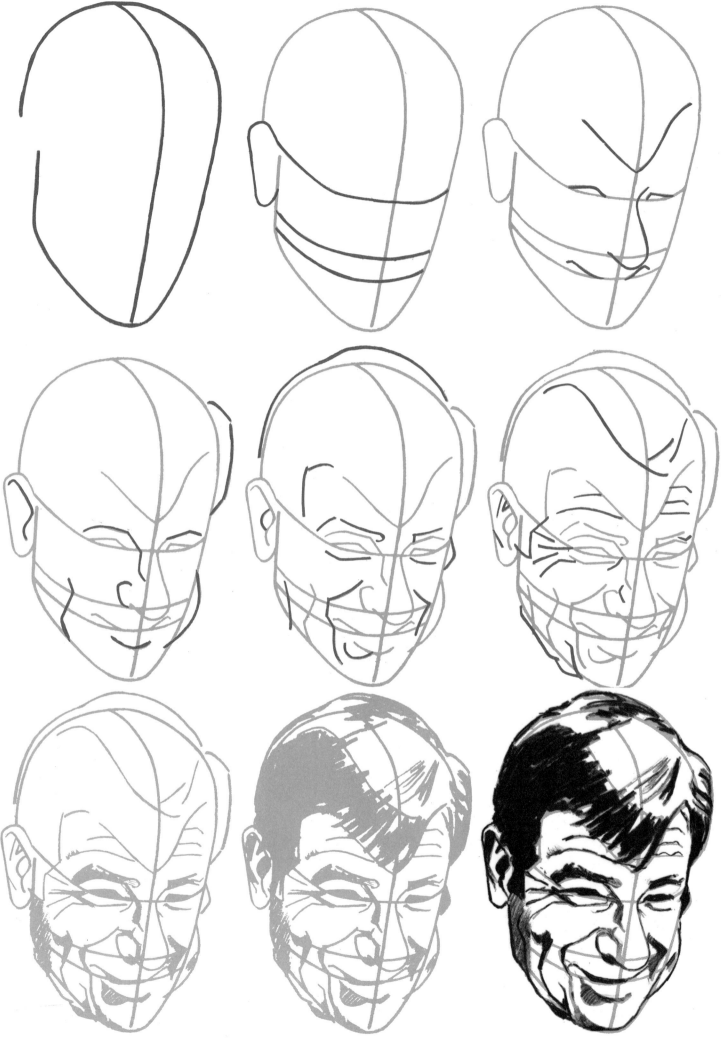

Walter Matthau

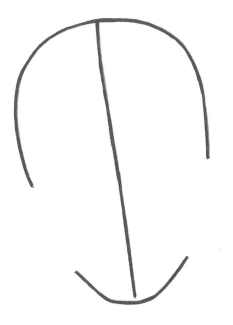
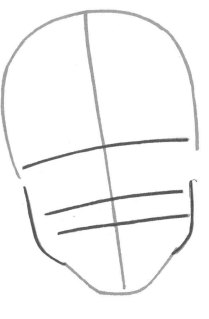

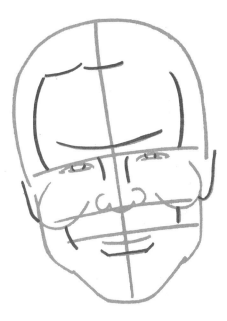
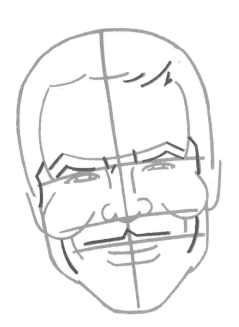

Burt Reynolds

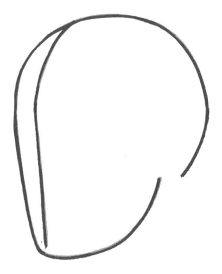
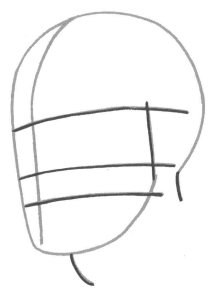
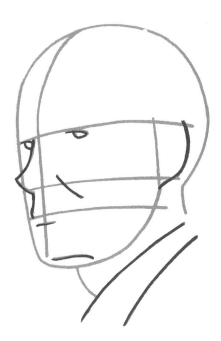
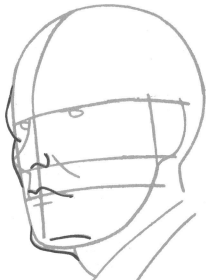

Clint Eastwood

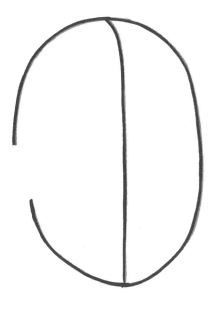
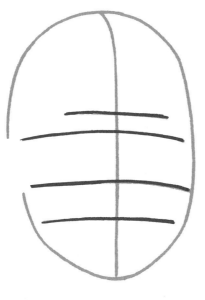
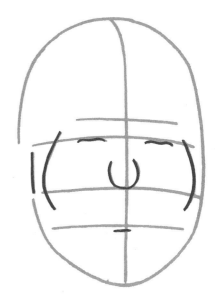
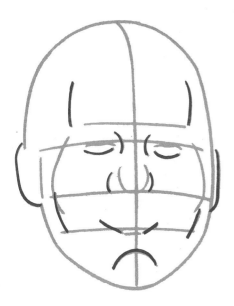
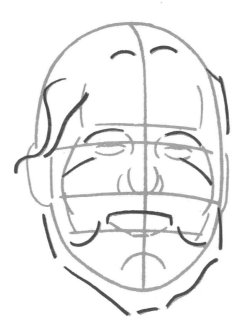

Kenny Rogers

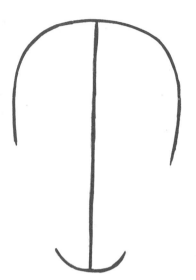
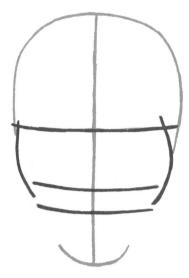
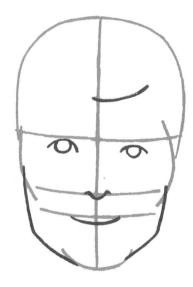

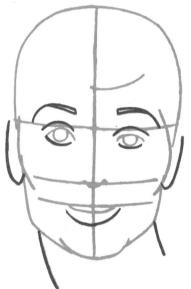
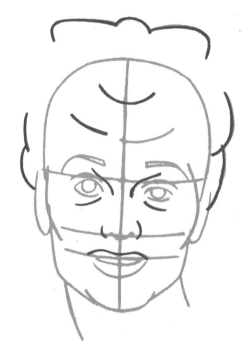
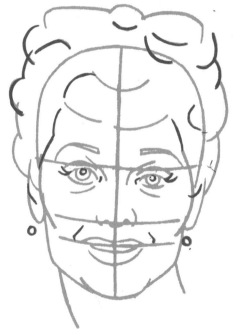

Lucille Ball

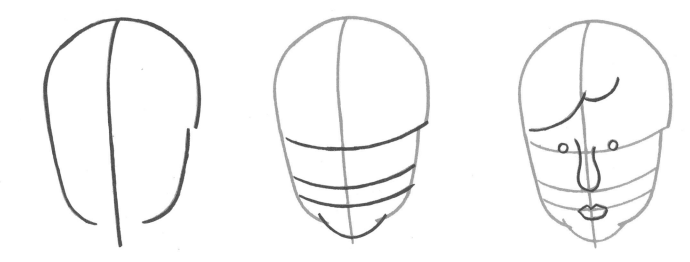

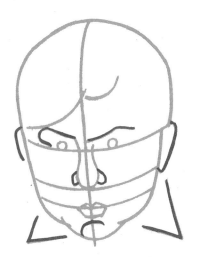

Hervé Villechaise

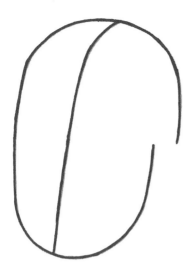
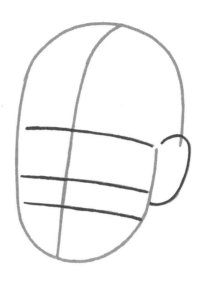
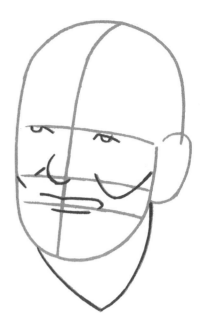

Alan Alda

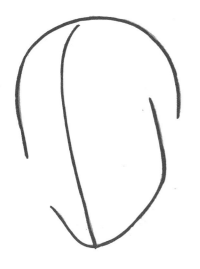
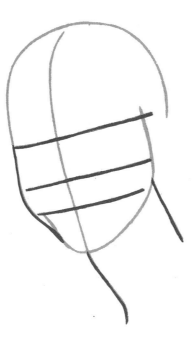

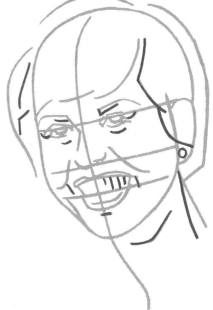

Marie Osmond

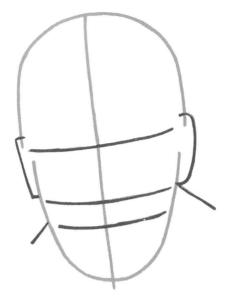

Jack Klugman

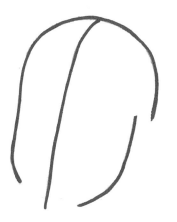
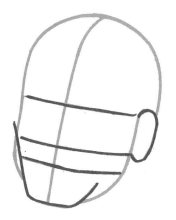

Robin Williams

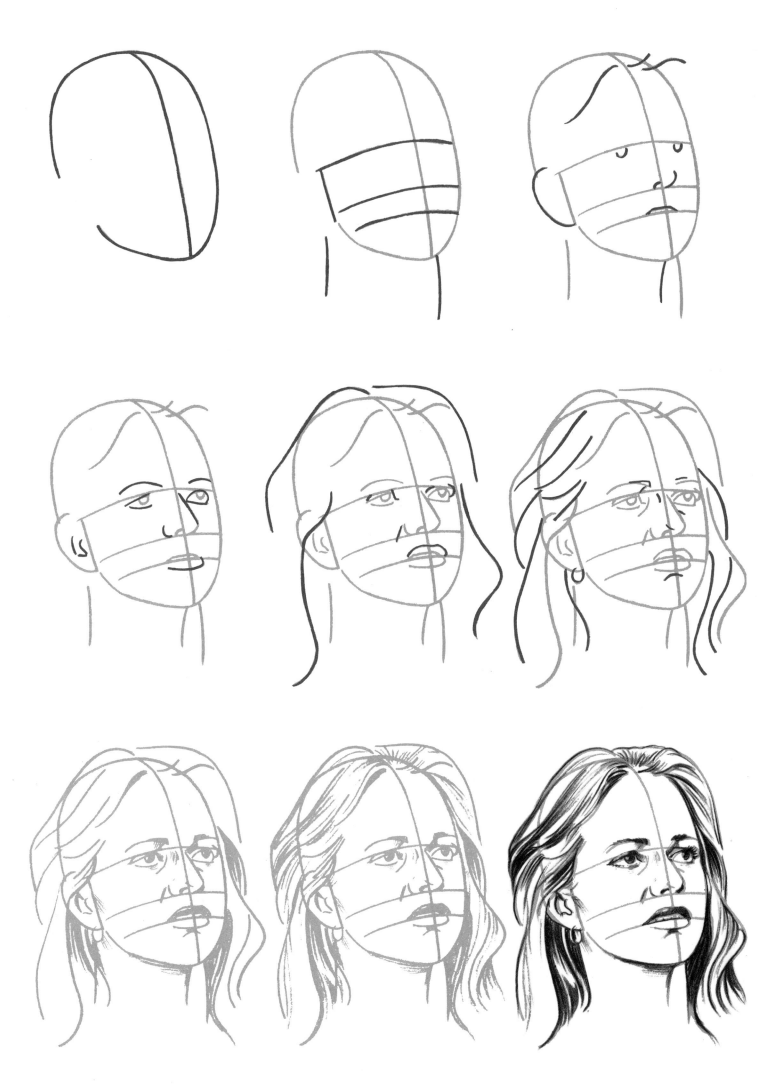

Sally Field

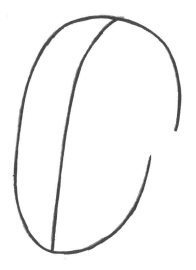
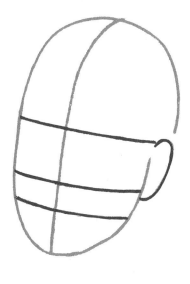
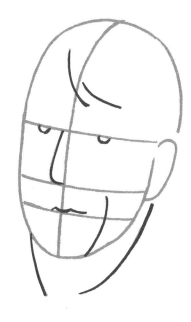
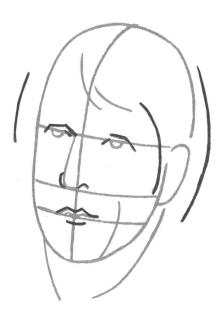

Dustin Hoffman

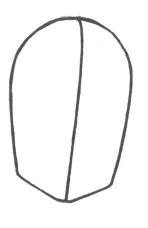

Loni Anderson

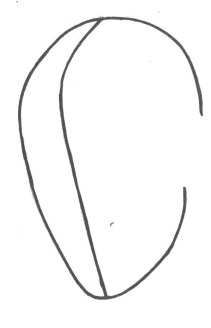

Elvis Presley

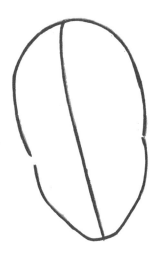
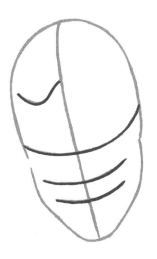
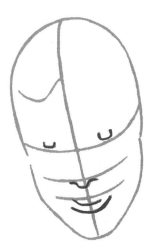
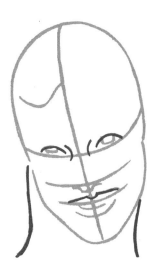

Brooke Shields

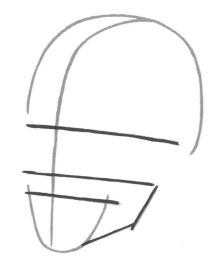

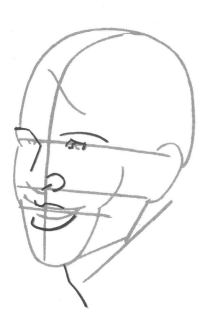

Warren Beatty

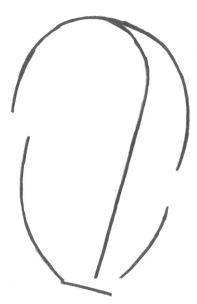
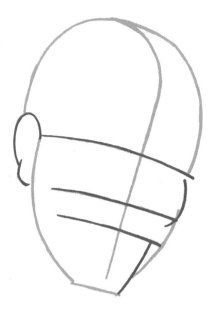

Sidney Poitier

Loretta Lynn

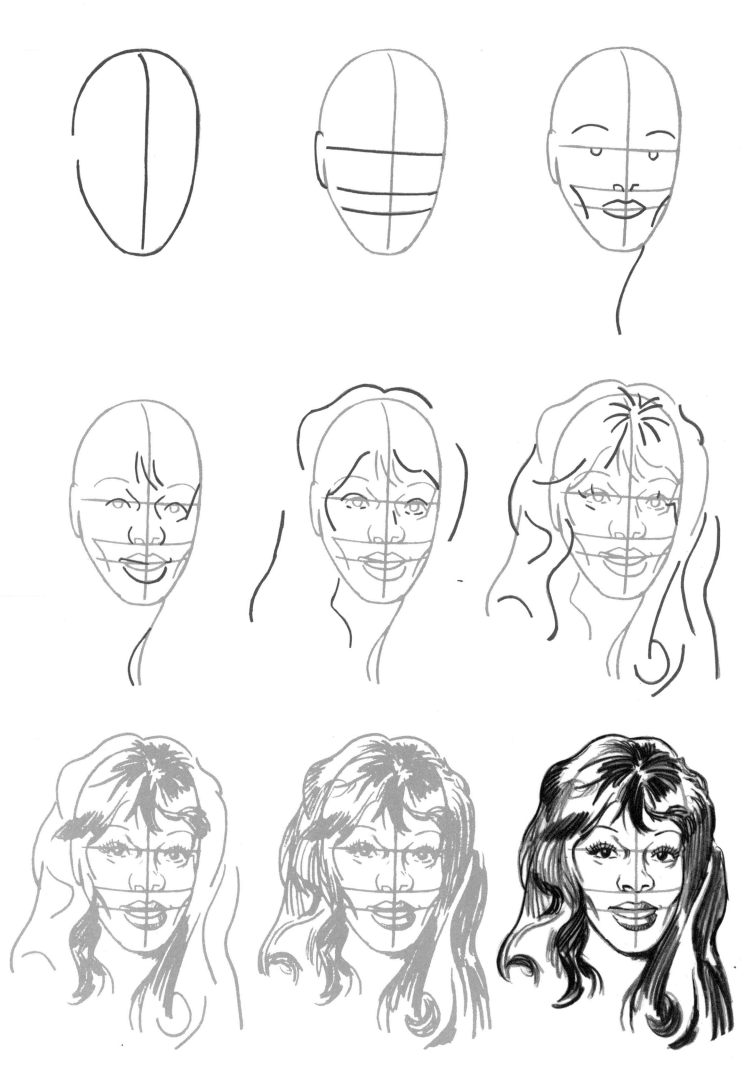

Donna Summer

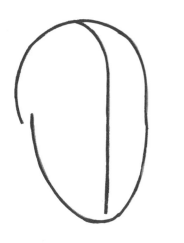
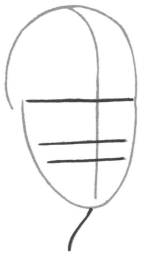
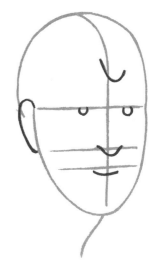
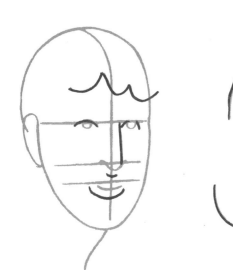

Bette Midler

Robert Redford

Sophia Loren

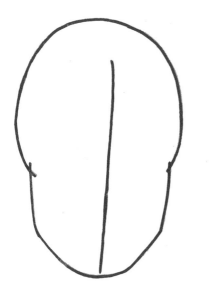
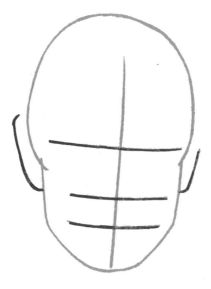
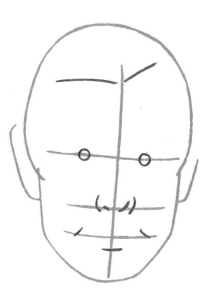

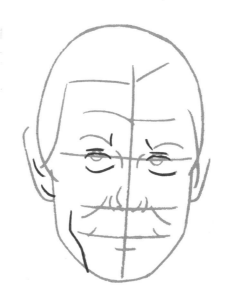

Johnny Carson

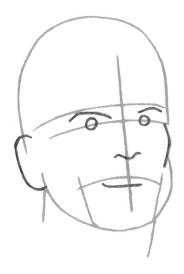
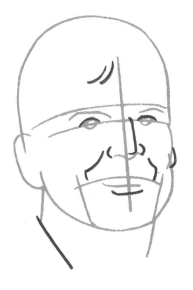
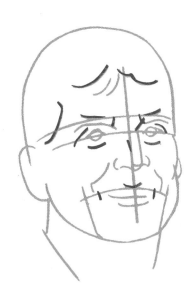

Erik Estrada

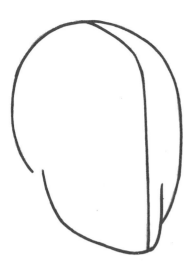
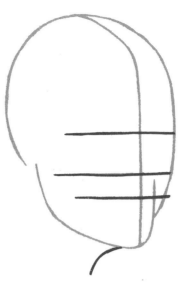
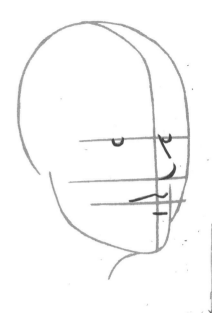
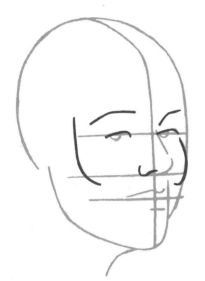

Carol Burnett

Woody Allen

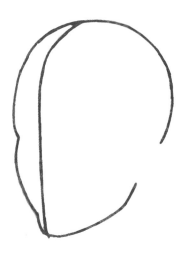

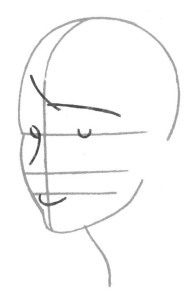
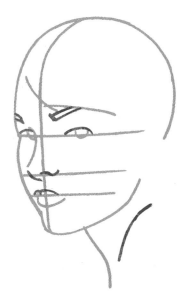
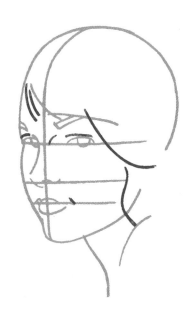

Valerie Bertinelli

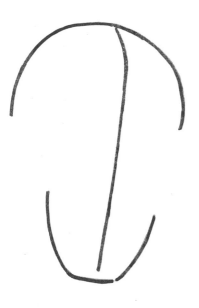

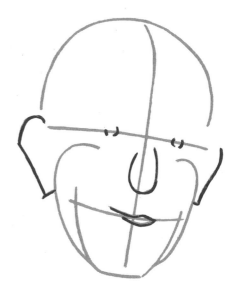

George Burns

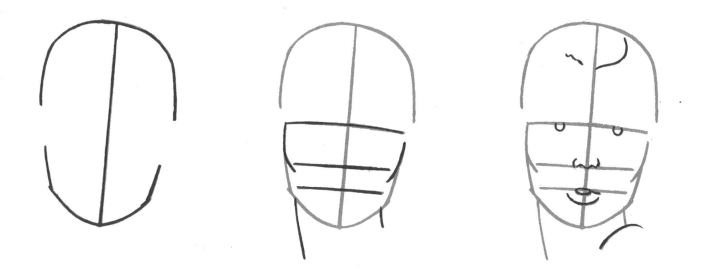

Marilyn Monroe

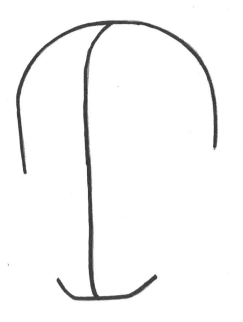
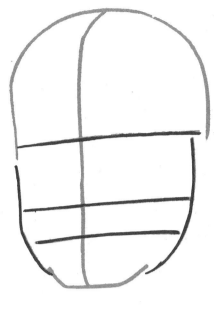
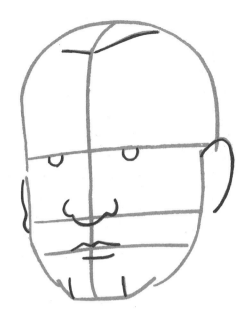

George C. Scott

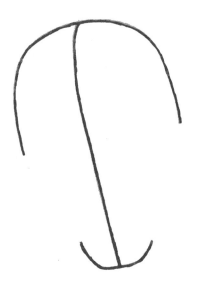

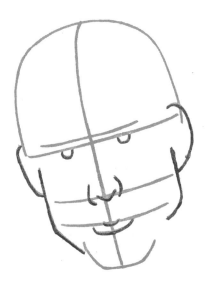

John Travolta

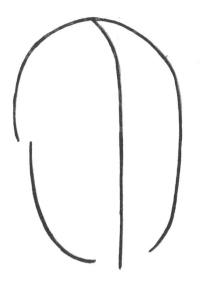
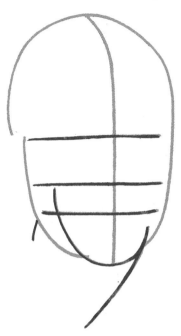
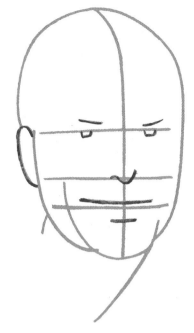
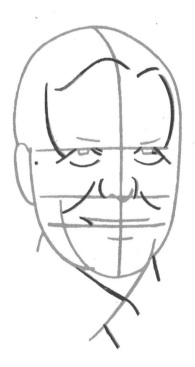

Robert Wagner

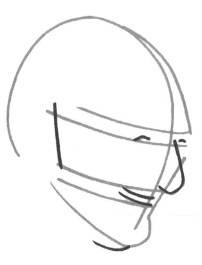

Liberace

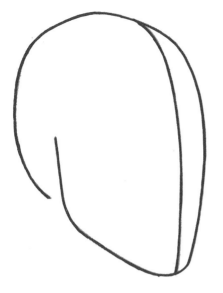
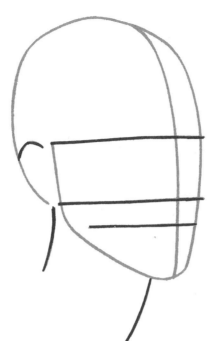
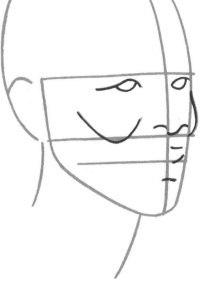
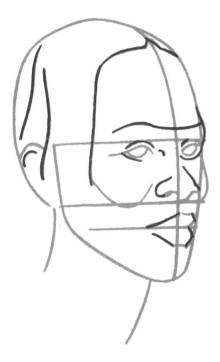
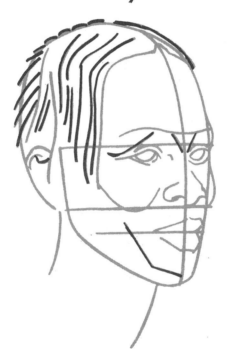
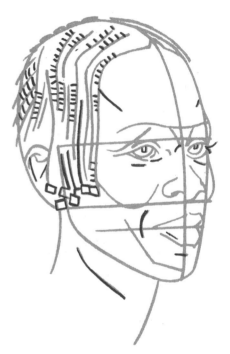
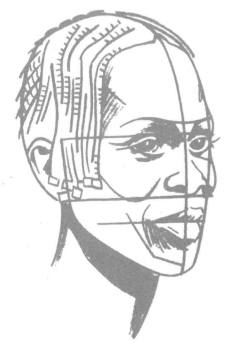

Cicely Tyson

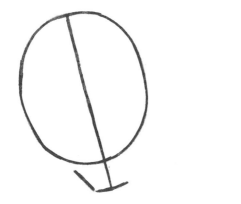

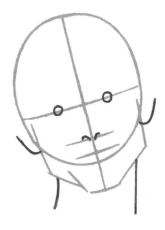

Valerie Harper

Lee J. Ames has been earning his living as an artist for more than thirty-five years. He began his career working on Walt Disney's *Fantasia* and *Pinocchio.* He has taught at the School of Visual Arts and, more recently, at Dowling College on Long Island. He was, for a time, director of his own advertising agency and illustrator for several magazines. Mr. Ames has illustrated over one hundred books, from pre-school picture books to postgraduate texts. When not working, he relaxes on the tennis courts. A native New Yorker, Lee J. Ames lives in Dix Hills with his wife, Jocelyn, their two dogs, and a calico cat.